the CHRISTIAN LIFE TRILOGY
CAMPAIGN MANUAL

Christian Life Trilogy Campaign Manual
Copyright ©2014 by Bible Study Media, Inc.
Printed in the United States of America.
All Rights Reserved.

ISBN # 978-1-942243-07-6

TABLE OF CONTENTS

INTRODUCTION	1
USING THIS MANUAL	4
CAMPAIGN OVERVIEW	5
YOUR ROLE AS SENIOR PASTOR	19
CAMPAIGN DIRECTOR	30
COMMUNICATION AND PROMOTION TEAM	35
PRAYER TEAM	39
SMALL GROUPS AND SUNDAY SCHOOL TEAM	47

1

INTRODUCTION

The ebb and flow of the Christian life is a rhythm of God's people moving back and forth from small group gatherings of fellowship, prayer, and study to larger group gatherings of corporate worship and celebration. All of the great missionary expansions of the Gospel involved just such movement—from small groups of Christians meeting together for mutual support, learning, and prayer to the larger corporate gatherings of praise and exhortation. Consider the example of the early church, recorded in Acts 2:42-47:

"And they devoted themselves to the apostles' teaching and the fellowship, to the breaking of bread and the prayers. And awe came upon every soul, and many wonders and signs were being done through the apostles. And all who believed were together and had all things in common. And they were selling their possessions and belongings and distributing the proceeds to all, as any had need. And day by day, attending the temple together and breaking bread in their homes, they received their food with glad and generous hearts, praising God and having favor with all the people. And the Lord added to their number day by day those who were being saved."

Notice the spiritual and numerical growth the early church experienced as a result of their mutual support and devotion. When Christians share their lives together with one another, the Lord Jesus manifests His presence among them—God is glorified.

In many ways, the small group meeting and the large gatherings on Sunday are interdependent, mutually beneficial to one another. The small group held in isolation from larger corporate worship can become isolated, unholy in its pursuits, and misguided by personalities and the whims of a few. In the same way, the large group gathering gains its passion and dynamism from the energy, accountability, and love fueled by small groups.

Bring the two together in a congregation and the Lord will add day by day those who are being saved—new life, new creation!

The *Christian Life Trilogy* seeks to foster the small group life of a congregation, but always with the aim and end of gathering the whole family back together in larger corporate worship and celebration. In this way, the series hopes to encourage a return to the things of first importance in the church—communal life and the heart of the message of the Church: Christ has died, Christ is risen, and Christ will come again. Therefore, we undertake this journey, following His command together to "remember His death, proclaim His resurrection, and await His coming in glory."

The structure of the series reflects the pattern and heart of the Christian life. Every year, we calendar our lives around Good Friday, Easter, and Pentecost, recognizing that Jesus' crucifixion, resurrection, and ascension form the heart of Christian belief and reveal the heartbeat of God for the people of God.

The first series of the trilogy, The Crucified Life, begins the Sunday before Ash Wednesday and calls the corporate body back to the central purpose of Lent, to pick up our cross and follow Jesus as His disciples. The teaching and reflections invite us into the daily process of dying to self in order that we might fellowship in His sufferings of Good Friday and thereby attain the joy of Easter—unity with the Christ in His glorious resurrection.

> **PRAYER FOR THE CHURCH:**
> "O God of unchangeable power and eternal light: Look favorably on your whole Church, that wonderful and sacred mystery; by the effectual working of your providence, carry out in tranquility the plan of salvation; let the whole world see and know that things which were being cast down are being raised up, and things which had grown old are being made new, and that all things are being brought to their perfection by him through whom all things were made, your Son Jesus Christ our Lord; who lives and reigns with you, in the unity of the Holy Spirit, one God, for ever and ever. Amen"
>
> **BOOK OF COMMON PRAYER**
> **PP. 280 (GOOD FRIDAY), 291 (EASTER VIGIL)**

But our new life doesn't end there. In many churches, Easter Day is a glorious celebration of worship; yet mysteriously, the church goes right back to the normal routine just as things are about to get exciting! Easter is meant to be more than just one day—it is meant to be an entire a season of hope and renewal. That's why the second in the series, The Resurrected Life, explores how everything changes in the light of Jesus' resurrection. Jesus says, "Behold, I am making all things new!"

INTRODUCTION

The activating and energizing power behind both the Crucified and Resurrected Life is the Holy Spirit of God. The Spirit-Filled Life, the third in The *Christian Life Trilogy*, explores the activity of the Holy Spirit calling us to Christ, gifting us for service, and pouring out the love of God in our hearts that we might carry that love to the world. Discover what it means to "walk in the Spirit" on a daily basis.

My hope and prayer for you and your congregation is that these materials would be used by God to bring the life of Christ to your church in an exciting new way. As you gather in small groups and in corporate worship, may the dynamism of the living God stir your hearts with His truth, fill you with hope, and equip you with power. I invite you on this unique walk through the Christian journey, from Crucified to Resurrected to Spirit-Filled Life!

–Rev. Charlie Holt

USING THIS MANUAL

As you begin to prepare and plan for your *Christian Life Trilogy*, it is our desire to clearly share what we have learned about doing spiritual growth campaigns. We firmly believe in the life-changing power and potential fruitfulness of this campaign because it will be the catalyst to help your congregation discover God's plan for Christian formation in the Church.

We've prepared this *Christian Life Trilogy* Campaign Manual as a reference tool to help you in planning and launching your campaign and maintaining healthy small groups in your church after the campaign. The materials in this manual are the byproduct of years of actually doing spiritual growth campaigns. From the men and women who implemented those campaigns come the very best principles and practices to share with you.

IMPORTANT: The Senior Pastor and Campaign Director should review all of the materials in the *Christian Life Trilogy* Manual to gain an understanding of the scope of the campaign and to begin to think through how to adjust the campaign to fit your church context.

Additional campaign resources and downloads are available at
http://www.christianlifetrilogy.com/resources.

5

CAMPAIGN OVERVIEW

We are glad you are joining us in the *Christian Life Trilogy* small group journey. Our prayer is that the Church will be transformed through this spiritual growth experience.

Your excitement and anticipation as you begin this experience is wonderful; but knowing you are leading your church into a place where God will reveal His plans for His people is even better. Too many Christians wander through life never realizing all that God has in store for them. Many never stop to think about how God desires to use His people. Others have no concept of the joy and fulfillment available to us as followers of Jesus. This spiritual growth experience offers the opportunity to understand God's heart for our spiritual development and what He has given for our use while we live here on earth as well as for the life to come.

STRATEGY OVERVIEW
The *Christian Life Trilogy* strategy will be:

1. **Prayer-Centered**

    - Making meaningful decisions by seeking God's will.

    - Praying: *Lord, what would you do through me to accomplish your will in my church?*

    - Thanking God for blessings and for the opportunity to make a difference in people's lives.

2. **Vision-Driven**
    - Always clear about a sense of God's calling. What does God want to accomplish in and through your members?

- Always about people. Creating a culture of growth and maturity as the Church grows up into Christ.

3. **Community-Based**
   - Authentic sharing and transforming growth occurs in the context of a safe, caring small-group setting. The early church followed this model, as Acts 2:46 states: *"And day by day continuing with one mind in the temple, and breaking bread from house to house, they were taking their meals together with gladness and sincerity of heart…"*

4. **Maximum Impact**
   - You will get maximum impact from your church-wide spiritual growth campaign when everyone in your church participates in each part of the campaign. Imagine the excitement when everyone is united, spending the church year together in both worship services and in small groups.

THE POWER OF ALIGNMENT

Coordinating and aligning the elements of the *Christian Life Trilogy* will impact and produce the kind of spiritual growth that will move your congregation from spectators to active participators in the Body of Christ. Imagine for a moment the impact on your church if every person lived in alignment with God's will in the areas of serving, growing, and even giving. What if your people lived in powerful community with their small group or Sunday School class? What if, as groups, people began to experience the power of God in their lives as an entire congregation? By making the most of the following three campaign components, you will see the power of God working in your church. These five components build from micro to macro, from a narrow scope to the broadest.

1. **Individual Participation**
   This is the real heart of the campaign, and it is the element that will produce the greatest spiritual growth among the members of your congregation. The goal is to get people to read and reflect on God's Word and consider His will for their lives daily throughout the campaign. By participating in this campaign, each person will be challenged to grow spiritually and experience God's plan for living a transformed life.

2. **Group Participation**
   A powerful element of the campaign is getting people to explore and experience God's will in true biblical community. We provide you with curriculum to be used in small groups or Sunday School classes for adults. Individuals bonded to a smaller community of believers within your congregation will enjoy the benefits of sharing life, spiritual growth, and accountability for that growth. These small group experiences are vital to ensuring the greatest personal spiritual growth as well as a commitment to ongoing growth as a community within your congregation.

CAMPAIGN OVERVIEW

3. Service Participation
The services that take place during the *Christian Life Trilogy* journey include Ash Wednesday, Holy Week, Easter, and Pentecost. These services offer opportunities for the Senior Pastor and worship planning team to further explore the lessons of the small group curriculum for your congregation.

CAMPAIGN PRINCIPLES

Prescription. Think of running your campaign like you would rear a child. While there are principles that are transferable, every child is different and every family is different. Similarly, every campaign is different. You know your church family, you know the structure of your church, you know the personality of your church, and you know the culture of your community. *we don't*. This material will be prescriptive, but you will need to be interpretive. We will tell you what we have done and what we feel are transferable principles, but you will have to contextualize the campaign to fit your congregation. It may not be realistic for you to attempt to implement all facets of the campaign. That's okay. Carefully and prayerfully consider how you need to shape this campaign to fit your church.

POWER THROUGH PRAYER.

Woven throughout this Campaign Manual is the repeated exhortation to release God's power through prayer. Prepare with prayer, plan with prayer, implement with prayer. Without prayer, this campaign could just be a series of exhausting activities. With prayer, this campaign is infused with the power to affect real change in people's lives.

RESULTS.

We are excited as we envision your entire congregation living God's purposes for their growth. This *Christian Life Trilogy* will empower your congregation and impact your community. Consequently, you will see maturity in the members of your congregation. The events of the campaign will give your church family opportunities to:

- commit to habits of spiritual growth and a personal devotional life,
- participate in a small group or Sunday School fellowship,
- memorize Scripture,
- learn to live a lifestyle of worship to the glory of God, and
- serve in a ministry in your church.

A byproduct of this *Christian Life Trilogy* is a solid, sustainable Small Group Ministry within your church. This growth will result in a more powerful church community.

THE CURRICULUM

God desires great things for our lives. His plan includes life with meaning and significance, a life with purpose, and a life without regrets. Most people believe their lives are good, but would they say they are experiencing God's best? What's the difference? The difference is the world's way versus God's way. That's what this curriculum is designed to help everyone in your church discover—God's plan for them. During this study, participants will look closely at their lives. They will consider whether they are pleased with what they discover about their lives, or whether at the end of life here on earth, they may have regrets. The *Christian Life Trilogy* is a journey toward taking hold of all God has planned for us.

The *Christian Life Trilogy* includes three curriculum titles:

The Crucified Life: The Seven Last Words of Jesus (Lent Season)

- Forgiveness: Father, forgive them for they know not what they do.

- Salvation: Today you will be with me in Paradise.

- Relationship: Woman, behold your son…Behold your mother.

- Distress: I thirst.

- Abandonment: My God, my God, why have you forsaken me?

- Reunion: Father, into your hands I commend my spirit.

- Triumph: It is finished.

The Resurrected Life: Making All Things New (Easter Season)

- All Things New: Overcoming Doubt and Fear

- New Life: Letting Go and Letting God

- New Temple: Inviting God's Presence

- New Body: Manifesting Jesus

- New Covenant: Experiencing Resurrection Power

- New Creation: Stewarding the Good News

- New Day: Living in the "Now" but "Not Yet"

The Spirit-Filled Life (Pentecost Season)

- Baptized: The Outpouring of the Spirit
- Adopted: The Calling of the Spirit
- Transformed: The Fruit of the Spirit
- Equipped: The Gifts of the Spirit
- Empowered: The Work of the Spirit
- Anointed: The Mission of the Spirit

CASTING VISION
God is at work around our country through the small group movement, sending a wave of spiritual renewal to the local church. He is using Small Group Ministry to grow His people and equip them to do the work of the kingdom both within the church and in the world around us. The key to all of this is vision casting. Almost every church wants to grow in numbers and reach out to its community. Vision casting is explaining the dream of Jesus Christ, that every sheep would have a shepherd, meaning that every believer would be connected to another so that the Body of Christ can fulfill its purpose. It's also giving your church body easy tools by which they can accomplish this. A Small Group Ministry campaign can do all of this at once. Additionally, such a campaign has some amazing fringe benefits, like growth in church attendance and giving, as well as building an effective network through which the Senior Pastor and staff can communicate to their church body. These fringe benefits help reluctant pastors, staff, and leadership see the value and purpose of being a church of small groups, not a church with small groups.

CATALYZE A MOVEMENT
In addition to discipleship and personal life transformation, launching a small group movement can build an increased sense of community among your congregation. Starting a small group movement can jump-start the sense of connection between church members. As a result, you can more effectively reach your community through the now deeper-connected members of your church. We recommend the following progression for accomplishing this:

1. First, connect your church members to small groups. Launching new groups and connecting your church members to these small groups is a high priority. One way to get more new groups to begin meeting is through a campaign—aligning a church-wide curriculum with the weekly sermons and encouraging participation in the study. The alignment provides incentive for the congregation to study the Senior Pastor's message more fully in their small groups and Sunday School classes. It provides an opportunity for the Senior Pastor to ask for people to host a new small group or lead a Sunday School class so that everyone can get connected. New group hosts and leaders can attract unconnected people they already know to be a part of their group—their family, friends, neighbors, coworkers, and others they meet on occasion.

2. Second, connect church attendees to small groups. Here, church attendees who are unconnected to others in the church can get connected. New group hosts and Sunday School leaders are recruited from the church membership to form new groups that will include people who respond to the "ask" during the weekly sermon—the "ask" for who would like to be part of a small group. Members of existing small groups can launch their own group for the *Christian Life Trilogy*.

3. Finally, connect your small groups to the community. New groups and current groups are encouraged to reach out to people outside the church in their neighborhoods, workplaces, etc., that they may or may not know well. New small group hosts are encouraged to hold a social event with a few family, friends, neighbors, coworkers, or others to pray about who they can ask to join their group, making lists, writing postcards or calling with a personal invitation to join the group.

SMALL GROUP MINISTRY LEADERSHIP MODEL
Developing a structure for leading your church's Small Group Ministry is an essential element in sustaining the small group movement in your church post-campaign. You will identify teams of Community Leaders and Coaches to oversee up to 5-10 small group hosts each (up to 50-100 people in groups of 10 people).

The positions of Community Leader and Coach help fulfill the mission of the church by:

1. Managing, ministering, and administering to the spiritual development of individuals and,

2. Encouraging the growth and expansion of their twenty or more small groups.

There will be more discussion on establishing and organizing your Small Group Ministry in the *Small Groups and Sunday Schools Team* section of this manual.

CAMPAIGN TIMELINES
The campaign timelines give you general guidelines for planning and implementing each part of the campaign. A suggested master timeline would involve:

- **The Crucified Life:** Ash Wednesday to Easter

- **The Resurrected Life:** Easter to Pentecost

- **The Spirit-Filled Life:** Launched either at Pentecost or in the following fall of the year.

WORD OF ADVICE: Begin your planning early and follow your plan in order to make the *Christian Life Trilogy* more enjoyable for everyone. When things are done at the last minute and people are stressed and frustrated, they are soon distracted from the purpose of the experience.

THE CAMPAIGN TEAM

Most leaders are used to putting together strategic plans, action plans, and to-do lists to quickly get a job done. In the same way, it would be easy to hastily recruit a team from people who are available. To yield the best results, however, prayerfully ask God to provide the right people for each task. As you begin to pray about whom God wants to be on your Campaign Team, He will reveal these individuals to you—sometimes people you had not thought of have the needed gifts.

Your Campaign Team is made up of committed leaders who each will lead a team to coordinate one or more of the components of the campaign. Their collective objective is to create opportunity and motivation for everyone in the church to join a small group for the *Christian Life Trilogy*, and then encourage them to stay connected in small groups after the campaign is over.

There is a segment of this manual dedicated to each Campaign Team Coordinator position. Each segment identifies characteristics for potential members of your teams as well as the type of gifts needed to be most effective in the role. For maximum impact, you will need to tap into the volunteer base of your church. The broader the base of involvement, the greater the ownership will be.

TEAM STRUCTURE

The Campaign Team described in this *Christian Life Trilogy* Manual is comprised of a Campaign Leader (the Senior Pastor), a Campaign Director, and Campaign Team Coordinators who, in turn, coordinate a team that carries out one campaign task.

These roles are the ideal. However, it may not be possible for you to fill every role with a dedicated person. Keep this in mind as you build your team and select what works for your church. You may find that combining some roles will be more effective for you.

Initially, hold team meetings monthly. Then, once you are nine weeks away from the campaign launch, step it up to meeting every other week. Finally, in the six weeks before the campaign and for the six-seven weeks of each study, it might be wise for your Campaign Team to meet weekly. Try to have your entire Campaign Team assembled well ahead of the campaign.

Tactical Considerations
Step-by-step procedures are given for implementing each phase of the *Christian Life Trilogy*. However, remember that these guidelines cannot be simply imposed upon your congregation. You need to evaluate each recommendation and decide whether it fits your church, factoring in your local context.

To recruit the best people for your team, you may need to anticipate releasing some of them from current key responsibilities at the church while serving on this Campaign Team. It is important to hold regular meetings and you don't want to ask too much of any one individual.

Build a strong sense of community within your team. Get to know one another and share your lives authentically. Mutually support one another, get down on your knees and pray together, dream and trust God together.

Team Descriptions
The Campaign Team is described below. Two key positions for overall leadership of the Campaign Team are the Senior Pastor and the Campaign Director.

Senior Pastor
The contribution of the Senior Pastor is to serve as the campaign leader. The campaign will not succeed if the Senior Pastor is not actively involved in the leadership and vision casting for the campaign. This strategic point of leadership for the campaign cannot be delegated. For more information on the role of the Senior Pastor, see Your Role as Senior Pastor beginning on page 19.

Campaign Director
Aligned with the Senior Pastor, the Campaign Director will provide overall leadership for the campaign. Working with the Senior Pastor, the Campaign Director develops the action plan using strategies that meet the goals of the campaign, oversees implementation of the action plan, and works with the Senior Pastor to recruit the rest of the Campaign Team. In addition, the Campaign Director does the following:

- Manages, supports, and provides leadership to each of the Team Coordinators.

- Coordinates team meetings.

- Manages (along with the Communication/Promotion Team Coordinator) the overall communication flow for the campaign.

- Secures photographers and videographers to record the events of the campaign.

- Coordinates with the Communication/Promotion Team Coordinator for production of print, email, and web materials related to the Campaign Director responsibilities.

- Prepares for and submits to an "interview" coordinated by the Communication Coordinator during a weekend service to answer questions about the campaign and communicate any needs for volunteers and prayer warriors.

The Campaign Director serves in a very visible role and must be a person who is supportive of and works well with the Senior Pastor. Effective planning and leadership by the Campaign Director in the early weeks and months will be crucial to the pacing and success of the campaign.

Some of the qualities that are desirable in the Campaign Director are:

- Catalytic leadership gifts;

- Strategic thinking with strong project management skills;

- Well-respected in the church;
- An authentic walk with the Lord; and

- Willingness to give the necessary time to this campaign.

For more information on the role of the Campaign Director, see the Campaign Director section beginning on page 30.

Administrative Team Coordinator
The Administrative Team Coordinator is responsible for developing and implementing strategies to support the connecting of members to small group hosts and Sunday School leaders, facilitating distribution of posters, flyers, handouts, email, bulletin inserts, etc., and working with all Team Coordinators to provide any administrative support needed to help make the campaign a success. This coordinator:

- Recruits staff and volunteers to help as needed to perform any administrative activities required of the various teams.

- Works with the Communication/Promotion Team Coordinator to facilitate delivery of print and email messages to individuals, groups, and leadership.

- Coordinates bulletin stuffing.

- Distributes materials to Community Leaders, Coaches, and small group hosts and Sunday School leaders.

- Maintains records on small groups and assists people in getting connected to a new group using software provided by the Campaign Director and Small Groups and Sunday School Team Coordinator.

The gifts and skills of your Administrative Team Coordinator should include:

- Good recruitment skills,
- Strong organizational gifts,
- Well-respected among your congregation,
- Knows the internal systems of the church,
- Ability to motivate, and
- A good communicator!

Communication/Promotion Team Coordinator
Your campaign needs a comprehensive communication plan that could include a broad range of strategies such as video, print, web, email, and signage. Your Communication/Promotion Team Coordinator will identify all points and avenues of communication in your church, produce the needed promotional materials, and oversee the implementation of all communications strategies. In addition, the Communication/Promotion Team Coordinator does the following:

- Prepares promotional content for Senior Pastor pulpit promotion, including video and PowerPoint.
- Recruits a dedicated communications team consisting of members with expertise in communication mediums of video, print, and web.
- Creates and delivers video promotion materials, graphic designs, printing, and web design for all of the other teams.
- Coordinates Communication/Promotion Team meetings.

The *Christian Life Trilogy* Manual contains several options that you could use. Here's what to look for in your Communication/Promotion Team Coordinator:

- Strong skills in video production, graphic design, and web production;
- Strong organizational gifts;
- Well-respected among your congregation;

- Knows the internal systems of the church;

- Ability to motivate; and

- A good communicator!

For more information on the role of the Communication/Promotion Team Coordinator, see the Communication/Promotion Team section beginning on page 36.

Prayer Team Coordinator
It is the Prayer Team Coordinator's job to implement prayer as a focus for the Campaign Team and develop and implement a prayer strategy throughout all of your church's ministries and age groups for the campaign. In addition, the Prayer Team Coordinator does the following:

- Recruits team members to implement the prayer focus and strategy of the campaign throughout the church in all age groups and ministries.

- Coordinates with the Communication/Promotion Team Coordinator for production of printed material, pulpit announcements, email blasts, signage, etc. related to Prayer Team responsibilities.

- Coordinates Prayer Team meetings.

The *Christian Life Trilogy* Manual provides prayer resources and materials to help the Prayer Team Coordinator infuse prayer into the campaign. When identifying your Prayer Team Coordinator, here are some characteristics to look for:

- Models a life of, and passion for, prayer;

- Well-respected as a spiritual leader;

- Marked by the character quality of perseverance;

- Can cast vision and motivate people to pray; and

- Well-connected to ministry leaders in the church.

For more information on the role of the Prayer Team Coordinator, see the Prayer Team section beginning on page 40.

Small Groups and Sunday School Team Coordinator
One of the most crucial goals of the *Christian Life Trilogy* is to promote group life and assimilate people into small groups or Sunday School classes. This is done through events

called "Connections," which take place at the start of your campaign. This is also done through sign-up opportunities at weekend services, through the web, and other methods your church has available.

Your Small Groups and Sunday School Team Coordinator will recruit the Small Group Ministry team and a sub-team that will develop and implement the plan for your Connection events. In addition, this team coordinator:

- Recruits, develops, and casts vision with a Small Group Ministry team to mobilize and motivate them.

- Recruits and develops a team that implements strategies and plans to orient, train, and lead small group coaches, small group hosts, and Sunday School leaders throughout the entire church for the duration of the campaign.

- Trains small group hosts or Sunday School leaders in the use of the *Christian Life Trilogy* small group curriculum.

- Identifies a method for tracking group leadership and membership and works with the Administrative Team Coordinator to implement it.

- Recruits, develops, and casts vision with a Connection Team to mobilize and motivate them.

- Coordinates with the Sunday Worship Team Coordinator regarding facilities needs for the church-wide Connection event.

- Coordinates with the Communication/Promotion Team Coordinator for production of printed material, pulpit announcements, email blasts, signage, etc. related to Small Groups and Sunday School Team responsibilities.

- Coordinates Small Groups and Sunday School Team meetings.

Some qualities to look for in the Small Groups and Sunday School Team Coordinator are:

- A heart for small groups and Sunday School;

- Good relationships with current leaders of groups;

- Outgoing personality with strategic planning gifts;
- Ability to problem-solve and delegate; and

- Ability to recruit new leaders and prepare them to effectively lead their groups.

For more information on the role of the Small Groups and Sunday School Team Coordinator, see the Small Groups and Sunday School Team section beginning on page 48.

Weekend Worship Team Coordinator
The person in this critical role works with the Senior Pastor, Campaign Director, and those who plan the worship services in your church to plan special features for weekend services, Connection events, and the Celebration event if applicable. This person looks for creative ways to help drive home the theme of each week's service. This can be done through testimonies, drama, video, Scripture readings, special music, banners, or numerous other means. This coordinator works with the Senior Pastor to implement and execute these powerful additions to the weekend service. In addition, this person, along with his/her team:

- Develops the Weekend Services Plan using strategies that meet the goals of the campaign.

- Coordinates with the Senior Pastor to align sermons with the small group curriculum by planning the message and timing of delivery to enhance the experience for participants.

- Coordinates with the Small Groups and Sunday School Team Coordinator regarding facility needs for the church-wide Connection event.

- Organizes and runs the church-wide Connection event.

- Coordinates with the Communication/Promotion Team Coordinator for production of printed material, pulpit announcements, email blasts, signage, etc. related to Sunday Worship Team responsibilities.

- Coordinates Weekend Worship Team meetings.

Ideally, this person has:

- Good planning gifts and creativity,

- Understanding of your congregation's worship style and what is appropriate in your church's context,

- A heart to assist the Senior Pastor in making the weekend service as effective as possible, and

- A commitment to excellence.

FIVE PHASES OF PREPARATION

Below is a sample timeline for the key tasks leading up to the campaign. Detailed timelines are provided to the teams by the Campaign Director once the date for your first *Christian Life Trilogy* sermon is set.

1. **Orient Yourselves**

    - Choose a Campaign Director.
    - Familiarize yourselves with the campaign.
    - Read the Campaign Manual.
    - Rally your key leadership.

2. **Set God-Sized Goals**

    - Pray and brainstorm about each area of the campaign.
    - Set goals only God can achieve.
    - Order resources.

3. **Recruit Your Team**

    - Recruit your Campaign Team.
    - Pray together.
    - Review the Campaign Manual together as a team.

4. **Develop Each Work Group**

    - Each campaign team coordinator assembles a work group team.
    - Each work group meets for orientation to their task.

5. **Plan and Customize**

    - Evaluate the campaign timeline for preparation, promotion, and execution of your campaign.
    - Customize the campaign for your church.

19

YOUR ROLE AS SENIOR PASTOR

Congratulations! You have begun an exciting journey by starting the *Christian Life Trilogy* and committing to a plan to encourage the growth of your congregation. As you start this journey, we are with you, side-by-side, praying for you and your congregation, for changed lives. As you begin, remember to keep the end in mind; that is, a flock of growing parishioners who do more than just attend services—they energize the church through their deepening spiritual passion and unity.

Your primary and most important role is presiding over glorious worship on Sunday morning and other weekend services and the Special holy days of Ash Wednesday, Holy Week, Good Friday, Easter Day, and Pentecost. As the chief liturgist of your congregation, plan these moments of corporate worship well. You have been trained for this. Lead and invite your congregation to the throne of Grace. As the small groups are meeting, God will be doing amazing work in the lives of the members of your congregation; that work must find expression and manifest corporately in word and sacrament, in spirit and truth.

Note: For those needing liturgical resources for Ash Wednesday, Holy Week, Good Friday, Easter, and Pentecost, one helpful resource is the Book of Common Prayer. It is in the public domain and available in Christian bookstores and online. It is free to be used and adapted for worship in any expression of Christ's Church. Visit http://www.bcponline.org.

You also have a central role as shepherd and pastor of your appointed flock. The materials and small group community will stir up pastoral work for you. People will be ready to take their hurt, fear, guilt and shame to the Lord. Be available to help them take those things to the cross of Jesus, pastorally and liturgically. They will be seeking to discern His unique calling for their lives. As their pastor, help them discern their spiritual gifts and their appointed ministry in the church and anointed mission to the world.

LEAD THE CAMPAIGN
As previously stated, the contribution you, the Senior Pastor, will make in the campaign is to serve as the leader. The campaign will not succeed if you are not actively involved in the leadership and vision casting.

Your first objective must be to help achieve a sense of ownership of the *Christian Life Trilogy* amongst the leaders of the church. It is a mistake to assume that approval by your church to participate equals buy-in by leaders and members. Willingness to have a campaign does not necessarily signify personal commitment to the campaign. Much of the resistance in churches comes when people have not been well informed and when they feel a new idea has been forced upon them. Keep this in mind as you approach your leadership.

ASK FOR PRAYER
Enlist people to pray for the campaign. Ask the elders and leadership of your church to begin praying now. Doing this will cast vision with the leadership and expand the possibilities of who might serve on your team. Also, ask your church leadership to begin asking God to reveal the right people to fill team member roles.

Support the Prayer Team in holding a Day of Prayer and Fasting—a time for all church leadership, campaign leadership, and staff to pause and pray for the campaign. Do this four weeks before the campaign launch, after the full Campaign Leadership Team is in place. Gather your leadership and staff together and ask them to fast and pray on a date you select.

IDENTIFY YOUR CAMPAIGN DIRECTOR
Your Campaign Director will align with you to provide overall leadership for the campaign. The Campaign Director will work with you to set goals and develop the campaign plan using strategies that meet those goals. For more information on the role of the Campaign Director, see the section titled Campaign Director on page 30.

You should choose your Campaign Director before you hold your initial Campaign Orientation Meeting, if possible, so that together you can develop the campaign strategies needed for a successful, measurable campaign.

DEVELOP CAMPAIGN STRATEGIES
Read the Campaign Overview section beginning on page 5 and work with the Campaign Director on developing each of the following strategies:

1. Determine the campaign start date. Consider the church calendar dates or holidays when planning the schedule. You can then create the Master Timeline to map out your campaign.

2. Determine the dates you will hold your Connections. We suggest three consecutive Sundays before the first sermon to recruit hosts and connect people into groups.

3. Set goals and a budget for the campaign.

4. Determine if video promotion and/or testimonies will be done to promote the campaign during the services.

5. Decide on the structure of your Small Group Ministry.

6. Decide whether or not you plan to allow members to sign up for groups on the web. If so, consider using a web-based small group tool. Ask the Small Groups and Sunday School Team Coordinator to evaluate current software such as ChurchTeams' online GroupFinder with built-in mapping software (www.churchteams.com). This will allow members to search for a group based on the day, time, and location that work best for them.

7. Decide if you will charge for curriculum up front or simply ask for donations. Be sure to budget for curriculum.

8. Map out the sermons that will be aligned with the *Christian Life Trilogy* small group studies.

9. Be prepared to suggest next steps for your small groups or Sunday School classes to take following the *Christian Life Trilogy*.

BE ON BOARD TO:

1. Review the Pastor's Training as well as resources at http://www.christianlifetrilogy.com to help you vision cast for the *Christian Life Trilogy*.

2. Maximize the impact of your services by synthesizing the elements of the campaign.

3. Sponsor a Campaign Orientation Meeting to rally and gain the commitment of your leadership.

4. Gather church staff and leadership to pray for the campaign.

5. Cast the vision of the campaign for your congregation and promote it from the pulpit.

6. Help recruit small group coaches and follow up with a thank-you to them.

7. Do the "ask" for small group hosts and Sunday School leaders from the pulpit at worship services.

8. Commission new small group hosts and Sunday School leaders during a worship service.

9. Do the "ask" for individuals to embrace the sermon series (that will be aligned with the curriculum) and to join with a small group for the duration of the campaign.

10. Promote your Connections from the pulpit.

11. Ask current small groups and Sunday School classes to take a break from their current studies to join the campaign study.

12. Model the way by hosting a group yourself.

13. Celebrate God's work, the small groups, and Sunday School classes at the end of the campaign.

Important: You will teach on the curriculum subject the week before the congregation studies the topic in their small groups or Sunday School classes. The expectation is that each small group will study the material the week following the sermon on that subject. You will introduce the next week's theme the next Sunday. For example, the theme of the first week of The Crucified Life is "Forgiveness," so the Sunday before Ash Wednesday would be Forgiveness Sunday. The theme of the first week of The Resurrected Life is "All Things New," so the theme of Easter Sunday would be All Things New.

EVALUATE AND SET GOALS

As you begin to set up the *Christian Life Trilogy*, take time to assess where you are right now. By taking time in the beginning to understand your current circumstances, you will be better prepared to build strategies that fit your church and that will result in accomplishing your goals for the long term.

On page 23 you will find a sample Assessment and Goals Worksheet. Look this worksheet over to discover the kinds of information you should evaluate pre-campaign. This information will help you set the goals and outcomes for your campaign in the areas of church attendance, small group involvement, finances, and ministry involvement. The worksheet provides space for you to assess the results in each area post-campaign as well.

ASSESSMENT AND GOALS WORKSHEET

As you begin to set up the Christian Life Trilogy, take time to assess where you are right now. By taking time in the beginning to understand your current circumstances, you will be better prepared to build strategies that fit your church, and wil (*text cut off here*).

1. Church Attendance:	Today	Post-Campaign Goal	Three Months Post	Six Months Post
Church Membership:				
Weekend Service Attendance (average):				
Youth Service Attendance (average):				
Children's Service Attendance (average):				
Number of Adults in Sunday School:				
Number of Youth/Children in Sunday School:				

2. **What is the current status and structure of your small groups?**
   These questions are to evaluate how many people you currently have in small groups and how many of your current resources (staff, volunteers) are involved in your small group ministry.

	Today	Post-Campaign Goal	Three Months Post	Six Months Post
Number of Adults in Small Groups:				
Number of Youth/Children in Small Groups:				
Number of Paid Staff:				
Number of Volunteer Staff:				

What is the structure of your small group ministry? _____

_____

_____

What are the strengths of your current model? _____

_____

_____

What are the areas to improve your current model? _____

_____

_____

3. What are the current financials of your church?	Today	Post-Campaign Goal	Three Months Post	Six Months Post
Giving (annually)				
Giving (weekly average)				
Budget (annually)				
Budget (weekly average)				
How many people are currently giving?				

4. **How many people are actively serving in the ministries of your church (List)?**

Ministry name	Today	Post-Campaign Goal	Three Months Post	Six Months Post

How many additional people serve seasonally, such as Christmas and Easter?	Today	Post-Campaign Goal	Three Months Post	Six Months Post
Ministry name				

5. **Do you have any daily devotionals, video streams, etc. which your church participates in?**

Type	Number

6. **When did you last have a spiritual growth campaign, or a dedicated time to connect your congregation into groups? How many have you done in the past 3 years?**

   Last stewardship campaign was: **In the past 3 years? (list:)**

   _____   _____

   _____

   _____

   What was the response? What worked and what did you hope would have had better results?

   _____

   _____

   _____

   _____

7. **What is the vision and mission of your church for the Christian Life Trilogy? How does what your church is actually doing match with your vision and mission for your church?**

   _____

   _____

   _____

   _____

SET YOUR BUDGET

It is important that you set an expectation for the cost of this campaign. To help you identify your budget items and estimate a budget for your campaign, we have developed a Budget Worksheet for your use.

Curriculum and Books	Qty. Needed	Cost per unit*	% Expected	Amount
The Crucified Life Devotional Book				
The Crucified Life Study Guide				
The Crucified Life DVD				
The Resurrected Life Devotional Book				
The Resurrected Life Study Guide				
The Resurrected Life DVD				
The Spirit-filled Life Devotional Book				
The Spirit-filled Life Study Guide				
The Spirit-filled Life DVD				
TOTAL				

*Quantity Discounts are Available. Visit http://christianlifetrilogy.com

COMMUNICATE THE VISION FOR YOUR CONGREGATION
One of the most critical factors affecting the success of the campaign is communicating the vision from the pulpit. Through testimonies and stories, you can share the vision of what you want for everyone in your church. Stories of life-transforming experiences in the individual members of your congregation have greater impact than any "ask" you can do.

Your own conviction to, and listing of, the benefits of being in a small group are key motivating factors to getting your people to join a small group for the campaign. When you say, "I am getting in a group too," the ripple effect is contagious. Everyone wants to "belong" …So jump on that bandwagon and use it to draw people in.

People won't grow further than you grow yourself. Participating in every aspect of the campaign yourself will be vital–reading the devotional books daily, memorizing the verses, and participating in a small group studying the *Christian Life Trilogy* curriculum. When you model God's teaching and live it out before your congregation, then the congregation will "get it." There is more power in your application of the truths of your sermon to your own personal struggle than there is in any great illustration or eloquent delivery.

MAXIMIZE THE IMPACT OF WEEKEND SERVICES
Work closely with your Weekend Worship Team Coordinator to maximize the impact of the services. The worship services during the campaign are powerful times that can harmonize the many elements of the campaign and underscore the curriculum in a memorable manner. Through the use of several tools designed specifically for the campaign, your services will become the time when the power of alignment comes into play, synthesizing the entire campaign for your congregation.

Ask your people to commit to the campaign. Don't discount the power of your pulpit. The pulpit is the rudder that steers the congregation. If there is any time to use your God-given authority in a way that urges people to spiritual growth, this is that time. Challenge people to jump into the campaign with both feet and commit themselves to the principles and the heart of the campaign. Foster a holy moment and ask your people to take the big challenge to make a big commitment. People are responsive to a personal challenge.

Hint: If you are the type of person who hesitates to ask big things of people, a campaign commitment card could be the tool you need at this juncture. You will talk through it during a sermon, asking your people to participate faithfully in the four major elements of the campaign–Scripture memorization, daily reading of the devotional book, worship service attendance, and small group or Sunday School class participation.

PASTOR'S MEETINGS
We suggest that you sponsor two meetings to kick off the planning and organization of your Campaign Team:

1. Campaign Orientation Meeting for Leadership. The first meeting is a dinner meeting for key church leadership, which you could call a *"Christian Life Trilogy* Orientation Meeting" or a *"Christian Life Trilogy* Briefing." It is important that you secure the commitment of your leadership up front. Hold this meeting at least 6-8 weeks before you would like to deliver your first sermon of the campaign. Commit an entire evening to the meeting so you don't feel rushed. In this meeting you will create ownership for the campaign, obtain commitment from your key leaders, and set the stage for a second meeting, described below.

2. Catch the Vision—Influencers Meeting. This second meeting, held about a week after the first, will include a broader scope of leaders in the church who have direct influence over the majority of the people in your congregation. It will also provide most of the people you need to take on Team Coordinator roles for the campaign (see the Team Descriptions in the Campaign Overview section of this manual for a list of these roles).

If you implement this strategy of meeting first with your key leaders and then with your entire team of official and unofficial influencers, it will help create the sense of ownership and commitment that is vital to the success of your church-wide spiritual growth campaign.

CAMPAIGN DIRECTOR

Welcome to the team! You have the great responsibility of recruiting and leading a group of coordinators and other volunteers in pursuit of a successful *Christian Life Trilogy* experience. This Campaign Manual should equip you with clear guidelines for your role and the roles of your teams.

Aligned with the Senior Pastor, you will provide overall leadership for the campaign. You will develop the action plan using strategies that meet the goals of the campaign. You will oversee the action plan and work with the Senior Pastor to recruit the rest of the Campaign Team. And you will manage, support, and provide leadership to each of the Team Coordinators. In addition, you will:

- Coordinate team meetings.

- Coordinate with the Senior Pastor and Weekend Worship Team Coordinator to align sermons to go along with the small group and Sunday School class curriculum.

- Report progress and challenges to the Senior Pastor and church leadership.

- Be a problem solver. Monitor and encourage all the Team Coordinators and help where necessary.

- Identify and budget for a photographer and/or videographer. If you are going to have a photographer and/or videographer at work before and during the campaign to capture the events and people on camera, you may want to book them early.

- Manage, with the Communication/Promotion Team Coordinator, the overall communication flow for the campaign.

- Coordinate with the Communication/Promotion Team Coordinator for production of print, email, and web materials related to the Campaign Director responsibilities.

- Review event planning with each event Team Coordinator using strategies that will meet the goals of campaign.

- Determine the standards and measurements of success and evaluate the success of the campaign.

You will also work with the Senior Pastor to accomplish the following:

1. Determine the campaign start date. Consider the church calendar dates or holidays when planning the schedule.

2. Determine the dates you will hold your Connections. We suggest three consecutive Sundays to recruit leaders and connect parishioners into groups.

3. Set goals and a budget for the campaign.

4. Determine if video promotion and/or testimonies will be done to promote the campaign during weekend services.

5. Decide on the structure of your Small Group Ministry. See the Small Groups and Sunday School Team section of this manual for information on a suggested Small Group Ministry Model.

6. Decide whether or not you plan to allow members to sign up for groups on the web. If so, consider using a web-based small group tool. Evaluate current software such as ChurchTeams' online GroupFinder with built-in mapping software (www.churchteams.com). This will allow members to search for a group based on the day, time, and location that work best for them.

7. Decide if you will charge for curriculum up front or simply ask for donations.

8. Determine a service project you will carry out as a church (to expand talent and use of time and resources).

9. Map out the sermons that will be aligned with the small group studies.

10. Prepare to suggest next steps for your small groups or Sunday School classes to take following the *Christian Life Trilogy*.

IMPORTANT: The Senior Pastor will teach on a subject the week before the congregation studies the topic in their small groups or Sunday School classes. The expectation is that each small group will study the curriculum material that week and then the next week's sermon will introduce the next theme.

The Team Coordinators you will need to recruit are:

- Administrative Team Coordinator
- Communication/Promotion Team Coordinator
- Prayer Team Coordinator
- Small Groups and Sunday School Team Coordinator
- Weekend Worship Team Coordinator

We've worked hard to make this as simple a process for you as possible. If you work through the manual, act in a timely manner, and get a solid team together, you should anticipate good results. Your effective planning and leadership in these early weeks and months will be crucial to the pacing and success of the campaign.

HOLD REGULAR MEETINGS
After you recruit your team, hold your first meeting. Communicate the main events timeline to the team and look over this Campaign Manual together to get yourselves on track. At the end of your meeting, spend time sharing your hearts for the campaign, praying for the team and the campaign, and committing to your next meeting date. We encourage you to spend time in the meeting working on each other's assignments together. This prevents isolation and promotes teamwork and accountability.

Begin holding team meetings right away with whatever team members have been recruited. When you are nine weeks away from the campaign, step it up to meeting every other week. Finally, in the five weeks before the campaign and for the six or seven weeks of the campaign, it might be wise for your Campaign Team to meet weekly.

Touch base with each of the Team Coordinators individually by phone or email every week to encourage, offer help, and pray with your team members.

COMMUNICATE THE VISION!
Communicate the Senior Pastor's vision for the campaign as well as the overall timeline, goals, and budget information with your Team Coordinators.

Each Team Coordinator should be encouraged to carefully review the Campaign Overview and the segment of this manual that relates to their area of responsibility. Do this right away!

CHOOSE YOUR TEAM
In the Campaign Overview, you will find descriptions of each of the required Team Coordinators. You probably already have an idea who you think would best fit each role. Pray over each role and choose people with characteristics similar to those found in those wonderful delegation passages in the Bible (Exodus 18 and Acts 6).

The Prayer Team's and Small Groups and Sunday School Team's responsibilities take more time than the other coordinator roles. Keep this in mind as you select your team.

ADMINISTRATIVE TEAM
Your Administrative Team is a support team for all the Coordinators to call upon to get administrative tasks done. In addition, this team will order curriculum, disseminate email and handout materials, coordinate bulletin stuffing, keep records on small groups formed, and connect individuals with groups. You will work with the Administrative Team Coordinator to see that these needs are accommodated.

COMMUNICATION/PROMOTION TEAM
Work with your Communication/Promotion and other Team Coordinators to design the overall church communication strategy for the *Christian Life Trilogy*. For example, you will need to look at the proposed communication strategies listed in the Communication/Promotion Team section of this manual on page 36 and decide together which elements you will use for your *Christian Life Trilogy*.

You will also need to determine whether you will use other strategies not suggested there so that Team Coordinators can facilitate their production needs with the Communications/Promotion Team.
For complete information on the roles and responsibilities of the Communication/Promotion Team, see the Communication/Promotion Team section on page 36 of this manual.

PRAYER TEAM

You will work with the Prayer Team Coordinator to encourage and monitor Prayer Team progress toward covering your *Christian Life Trilogy* in prayer. The importance of this cannot be overstated if your campaign is to be God-centered, as it should be. The management of the day-to-day tasks required to carry out the prayer emphasis will fall to the coordinator you have selected.

For complete information on the roles and responsibilities of the Prayer Team, see the Prayer Team section on page 40 of this manual.

SMALL GROUPS AND SUNDAY SCHOOL TEAM

The Small Groups and Sunday School Team will need your encouragement and guidance more than any other single team, as this team's responsibilities are great. This team will identify small group coaches, small group hosts, and Sunday School leaders. They will train and encourage them, provide for curriculum and other resources, and coordinate and monitor promotion of the small group Connection events.

For complete information on the roles and responsibilities of the Small Groups and Sunday School Team, see the Small Groups and Sunday School Team section on page 48 of this manual.

WEEKEND WORSHIP TEAM

The weekend services leading up to and during your *Christian Life Trilogy* are powerful tools that can be used to pull together the many elements needed to drive the message home in an effective manner. Through the use of several specifically designed tools, your weekend services will see the power of alignment come into play, synthesizing the entire experience for your church and community. You can use a variety of tools to help make your weekend services more effective. Your task as Campaign Director will again be to encourage the team and monitor progress.

CAMPAIGN TIMELINES

Throughout this manual we talk about timelines for the events of the campaign. You will need to provide actual timelines to each Team Coordinator once the Master Timeline has been set up.

You can find a sample Campaign Timeline which you may download and customize for your congregation's campaign at www.ChristianLifeTrilogy.com/resources.

COMMUNICATION AND PROMOTION TEAM

The Communication and Promotion Team will be pivotal in overseeing the production and delivery of each piece of communication for the campaign. Your campaign needs a comprehensive communication plan that could include a broad range of strategies such as video, pulpit announcements, bulletin inserts, bulletin announcements, response cards, email, flyers, banners and signage, and promotional postcards. As the Communication/Promotion Team Coordinator, you will identify all points and avenues of communication in your church, produce the needed promotional materials, and oversee the implementation of all communications strategies. In addition, you will:

- Coordinate with the Senior Pastor, Campaign Director, and Weekend Worship Team to implement weekend service strategies.

- Prepare content for pulpit promotion, including video and PowerPoint.

- Recruit a dedicated Communications Team consisting of members with expertise in the mediums of video, print (bulletin, handout, signage, email), and web.

- Create and deliver video promotion materials, graphic design, printing, and web design for all of the other campaign work groups.

- Coordinate Communication/Promotion Team meetings.

How to Communicate the Campaign
One of the challenges for the Communication/Promotion Team is to adequately and thoroughly communicate the campaign to your church family and community. When people don't understand something, they're more likely to be critical.

There are several key components in the *Christian Life Trilogy*, and it will be the responsibility of your team to prepare the materials to inform, promote, and motivate your congregation to be involved.

TACTICAL PRINCIPLES FOR COMMUNICATION

Principle 1. It doesn't have to be flashy, expensive, or high-tech to grab attention.

Without being elaborate or lavish, your communication can be well done and have a professional feel to it. Be clear in what you communicate, but also be creative. As a team, get your heads together and think of fun, diverse, unexpected ways that you could communicate this campaign to your congregation. Think outside the box. Brainstorm. Start with this question: If we couldn't use our weekly bulletin, the pulpit, or a newsletter, what would be the most effective ways to communicate this campaign to our people?

Warning: As you get creative, don't lose the clarity of your message. When introducing something new, it is more important to be clear than clever. Remember, the goal is for people to get the information, not to be impressed with your creativity.

Principle 2. Find as many times and ways to communicate as possible.

One widely known law of advertising is that a message must be communicated seven times before it really sinks in. One of the dangers is to assume that because you are familiar with something, others are also. When you think you are communicating adequately, double your efforts. Remember, you cannot over-communicate!

Principle 3. Clear the path for the *Christian Life Trilogy* to succeed.

If this campaign really is your church's program for Lent, Easter, and Pentecost, then you will have to help ensure that it receives proper priority in your church communication. You will want to be certain that all groups in your church know the dates for the campaign and are making necessary adjustments.

Principle 4. Communication is not just an activity; it is an attitude.

COMMUNICATION AND PROMOTION TEAM

One of the most effective communication devices at your disposal is your own attitude. It is imperative that the Senior Pastor, the Campaign Team, and your Communication/Promotion Team have a kind of contagious enthusiasm for what is coming. It is crucial for the Senior Pastor to champion the campaign from the beginning. As the Senior Pastor demonstrates and talks about his or her own commitment and involvement, the value of the campaign rises. Don't be afraid to utilize the weekend services to ask for commitment and participation from the congregation.

BUILDING YOUR TEAM

The communications strategy is carried out by a Communications Team using contact points throughout your congregation. The team consists of people with gifts and skills in communications, and the contact points include liaisons and email.

Team Size: This is definitely not a one-person job. Prayerfully recruit a full complement of team members. The size of your team will vary depending on the size of your church. Get as many people as you need to spread the workload, but not so many that it becomes complicated to manage.

Team Member Skills: Select team members who bring a good working knowledge of various communication media like print, video, web, and email. It is also helpful to have team members who understand all segments of your church and the existing communication avenues that are used, if possible.

PRAY

Encourage your team to pray at every opportunity during planning and executing the events of the campaign.

BUILD A COMMUNICATION STRATEGY

You will need to communicate with many groups to accomplish the task of communicating the campaign to your church and community. Establish a communication liaison in each of the campaign teams. This will likely be the Team Coordinator or a designee. These liaisons will be your contacts for communicating with each team. This will assure communication throughout the Campaign Team.

We recommend that you use a multi-tiered communications strategy that employs a combination of verbal, written, and graphic tools to keep people informed about the events of the campaign.

You may decide as a communications strategy that you want to use more bulletin announcements, inserts, or handouts; or you may feel that, in your church context, it would be helpful to use all communications avenues. It is advisable for you to lay out all the bulletin announcements, handouts, and bulletin inserts, and collate them with the pulpit announcements for each week, then decide what your best communications options will be.

COMMUNICATING WITH THE CONGREGATION

At the beginning of the campaign, it is important to give people ample opportunity to understand what you are doing and why. Don't worry about talking about the campaign too much. The more you communicate, the more people will become interested and feel comfortable with what may be some very new concepts.

Video: Consider using videotaped testimonies or movie clips to help bring home the message in the weekend services.

Web: Build a website to promote the campaign. Determine what web design is needed for the campaign and how you will accommodate both host and member signup for groups, if applicable. Web strategy ideas include:

- Post all information on the website to announce events, themes, and prayer requests.

- Research other church small group websites for ideas.

- Enable online small group sign up (online GroupFinder software on ChurchTeams. com).

DISTRIBUTION METHODS

In addition to the communication strategies listed above, you already have the two most important communication tools that you need: networks of relationships and existing communication channels. Work hard to identify all the various ways that information gets communicated in your church. Many ministries have developed their own systems of communicating with their people. Tap into the current systems and maximize their use.

Work with the Administrative Team for the distribution of the materials you produce. They are standing by with volunteers ready to stuff bulletins, send email announcements, and staff an Information Table. You may wish to make handouts available at an Information Table after they are initially distributed, in case people missed them.
The Administrative Team should start collecting all the email addresses in your church right away. While you cannot rely on email alone for communication, it is a quick and efficient means of keeping in touch with a significant portion of your congregation. Work with the Administrative Team to have emails sent out.

PRAYER TEAM

Pray that the Master's Word will simply take off and race through the country to a groundswell of response, just as it did among you. **2 Thessalonians 3:1 (MSG)**

The pinnacle of a Fourth of July celebration is the fireworks display. People of all ages flock to them to be reminded of what the United States of America overcame to secure its freedom. What a display!

Could your team trust God to use this spiritual growth experience to set off some spiritual fireworks in the house of God among the people of God? When prayer touches the fuse of God's power, spectacular things can happen!

Authentic spiritual transformation in your congregation and lasting Kingdom fruit in your community will not happen apart from prayer. A mighty movement of God's Spirit in churches cannot be realized by great plans alone. It is prayer that will bring to bear the power of God on the *Christian Life Trilogy*.

The Prayer Team will consist of a dedicated group committed to praying for the church-wide *Christian Life Trilogy* and to get everyone involved in praying for the campaign. The objective is to pray for God's will and acknowledge that, with His power and strength, all things can be accomplished.

PRAYER TEAM COORDINATION

As the Prayer Team Coordinator, your job is to implement prayer as a focus for the *Christian Life Trilogy* experience. In addition, you will:

- Recruit team members to implement the prayer focus and strategy of the campaign throughout the church in all age groups and ministries.

- Coordinate with the Communication/Promotion Team Coordinator for production of printed materials, pulpit announcements, email blasts, etc. related to Prayer Team responsibilities. Set up separate prayer sessions to support the goals of the church-wide small group launch.

- Coordinate Prayer Team meetings.

- Attend and lead prayer in campaign team meetings, when possible.

THE PRIORITY OF PRAYER

"Whenever God determines to do a great work, he first sets his people to pray."
–C.H. Spurgeon

Declare your need and dependence upon God. Looking ahead to the scope of the *Christian Life Trilogy* can be overwhelming. It can lead to feelings of inadequacy, fear, or stress. Let God use those feelings to bolster your faith and confidence in Him.

View prayer as the centerpiece of preparation for the campaign. In order for prayer to be the centerpiece of the preparation for the *Christian Life Trilogy*, it must be a central focus for the entire team, not just the Prayer Team. There are many tasks to be accomplished over the next few months to prepare for this small group campaign. Don't forget that perhaps the single most important preparation is that which takes place in the quietness of your prayer closet. Those who lead this experience must prepare personally through prayer.

Be aware of these prayer deterrents:

- Allowing the urgent (tasks and meetings) to crowd out what's important (prayer);
- Good intentions without a plan;
- Viewing prayer as nice but not necessary;
- Dry, mechanical, passionless prayer;
- Lack of modeling from leadership; and
- Lack of perseverance and faith.

JUST DO IT!

Churches are filled with people who do not need more training on prayer. They just need to pray. Churches need a Nike strategy—*JUST DO IT!* This is not about having prayer meetings where 45 minutes are spent sharing prayer requests and then three minutes are spent in prayer. Rather, this is about getting serious in prayer and calling upon God to do a great work.

A NOTE FROM OUR TEAM TO YOURS: The last thing we want to do is to heap guilt on you or your people. As Christians, we often have feelings of inadequacy or failure when it comes to our prayer lives. Prayer can be marginalized by long meetings, endless tasks, and mounting deadlines, and our good intentions can soon turn to regret. We all have much to learn about prayer, so we want to be proactive about becoming people of prayer. It is our desire that this *Christian Life Trilogy* deepens your faith and your faithfulness in prayer.

SEIZE EVERY OPPORTUNITY TO PRAY

- Spend significant time during your meetings in prayer.

- Gather a handful of people before or after a weekend service to pray.

- Pray in your small group or Sunday School class.

- Pray when you have a few minutes alone: in your car, at lunch, before going to sleep, just after waking, etc.

- Start praying with your children for the *Christian Life Trilogy* campaign.

The possibilities are limitless. You don't need extra meetings to have a strong focus on prayer.

A good plan is the engine of the *Christian Life Trilogy*; prayer is the fuel.

DON'T UNDERESTIMATE GOD'S POWER

Don't expect everyone in your church to be excited about or involved in the prayer focus. Be willing to start with just a few. But also don't underestimate what God can do through just a handful of people who fervently pray. Take heart, it takes just a little faith and a few people to move mountains.

In Luke 18, Jesus tells the story of a widow who came to a judge with a request for justice. Each time she came, the judge refused her request. But she just kept getting up each day and getting in line to bring her request. Finally, the Bible says, the judge answered her request so she wouldn't bother him anymore.

Here's the point: If an evil, mean-spirited judge would grant a request because of this widow's persistence, how much more does your heavenly Father delight to grant your requests when you persevere? So, get up each day and get back in line and bring your requests to the Father. Don't give up and don't give in!

LEAD BY MODELING
Prayer is more caught than taught.

- Commit to more prayer time personally.
- Talk about prayer, and its value, to others.
- Be excited about the difference that prayer can make.
- Challenge and enlist others to pray.

BUILDING YOUR TEAM

1. Decide who you will ask to be on your core Prayer Team.

- Form an extended prayer team of current ministry leaders and volunteers to pray for the *Christian Life Trilogy* on a regular basis.
- Consider the current prayer warriors in the church.

2. Motivate ministry leaders to pray for the *Christian Life Trilogy*.

- Host a Day of Prayer and Fasting for the church staff, Campaign Team, and ministry leaders. Ask the Senior Pastor to assemble the people for this.
- Ask the Senior Pastor to periodically gather the staff to pray for the *Christian Life Trilogy* campaign.
- Provide small group hosts and Sunday School leaders with weekly prayer requests.
- Ask church pastors and leaders to visit small groups and Sunday School classes to pray with them about the *Christian Life Trilogy*.

3. Motivate the entire church to pray for the *Christian Life Trilogy*.

    - Hold a church-wide prayer event (prayer vigil, prayer meeting, etc.).
    - Use vision dinners, training sessions, and every opportunity/venue to request prayer.
    - Hold a weekly prayer meeting on the church campus.
    - Use visual reminders for people to pray.
    - Motivate current small groups and Sunday School classes to pray for the campaign.
    - Motivate individuals to get a prayer partner for the *Christian Life Trilogy*.

4. Disseminate prayer requests and prayer meeting reminders.

    - Gather prayer requests from the Campaign Teams and hand them out to the church staff, Campaign Team members, and ministry leaders.
    - Use bulletin announcements, PowerPoint, and pulpit announcements.
    - Use email and existing prayer venues that already exist in your church.

5. Ask the Senior Pastor to pray from the pulpit.

    - Pray for the campaign leadership.
    - Pray for the commissioning of the small group hosts and Sunday School leaders as they launch new groups.

HOLD REGULAR MEETINGS

After you recruit your team, hold your first meeting. Communicate the main events timeline to the team and look over this Campaign Manual together to get yourselves on track. At the end of your meeting, spend time sharing your hearts for the campaign, praying for the team and the campaign, and committing to your next meeting date. Begin holding weekly team meetings right away with whatever team members have been recruited.

THE PLAN FOR PRAYER IN THE CAMPAIGN
As a Prayer Team, begin to carefully consider some of the following questions:

- What are the needs of our congregation that we can pray for?

- What are we asking God to do in us and in our church during the *Christian Life Trilogy*?
- How can we pray for our Senior Pastor and the other leaders in our church?

- What are some strategies that could help pockets of people throughout our congregation engage in prayer for the campaign?

- What are we trusting God for that is God-sized?

DEVELOP A MULTI-TIERED APPROACH
Develop strategies that:

- intensify prayer among the Campaign Team and in your corporate church services,

- foster prayer in your small groups, and

- encourage individual prayer.

Your prayers are plowing the spiritual soil of your church and preparing the ground for the coming harvest of changed lives. Jesus said, without God, it is utterly impossible. But with God everything is possible (Mark 10:27). Pray and then trust God.

Use the following checklists as a guide to develop your own ideas for infusing prayer into the structures of your church in preparation for and throughout the *Christian Life Trilogy*. Check the ideas that would work in your church setting, and write your own ideas in the blank spaces.

CAMPAIGN TEAM STRATEGY

- Hold a Day of Prayer and Fasting, a time for all church leadership, campaign leadership, and staff to pause to pray for the campaign. Do this about four weeks before the campaign launch after the full Campaign Leadership Team is in place. Gather your leadership and staff together and ask them to fast and pray on a date you select.

- Email or hand out a weekly prayer update with new requests each week.

CORPORATE STRATEGY

- Using a church-wide prayer focus, place prayer verses and prayer requests in the bulletin each week.

- Hold prayer times before, during, and after weekend and midweek services.

- Use prayer testimonies in weekend services to encourage prayer.

SMALL GROUPS AND SUNDAY SCHOOL CLASS STRATEGY

- Place a Prayer Tent Card in plain view at each meeting to remind the group to pray for the *Christian Life Trilogy*.

- Ask small groups and Sunday School classes to dedicate five to ten minutes each week to prayer for the *Christian Life Trilogy*.

- Pray each week for the *Christian Life Trilogy* activities and results.

- Encourage groups to memorize and meditate on a verse that will stimulate prayer.

- Have each group adopt one *Christian Life Trilogy* team member to pray for (by name or function).

INDIVIDUAL STRATEGY

- Distribute the Prayer Reminder Cards to the congregation to remind them to pray through *Christian Life Trilogy* goals and objectives.

- Commit to praying daily for the *Christian Life Trilogy*.

- Find a prayer partner to meet with at least weekly to pray for the *Christian Life Trilogy*.

PRAY FOR YOUR PASTOR AND CAMPAIGN TEAM

While it is exciting to think of your congregation discovering God's desires for stewardship in their lives, it would be naive to think that this will happen without resistance and spiritual warfare. So, be sure to provide a covering of prayer for those who will lead the *Christian Life Trilogy* campaign. Consider asking your Senior Pastor if you could have the privilege of putting together a special prayer team to pray for him or her during the *Christian Life Trilogy*. As Aaron and Hur held up the arms of Moses in the midst of the battle, this special prayer team would spiritually support your Senior Pastor as he leads the church through the *Christian Life Trilogy*.

IF YOUR SENIOR PASTOR GIVES PERMISSION, THEN FIND PEOPLE WHO:

- your Senior Pastor is comfortable with being on this prayer team,

- will faithfully pray,

- can be trusted with confidential requests should your Senior Pastor choose to share them with this group, and

- love and support your Senior Pastor and family.

"There is no power like that of prevailing prayer. It turns ordinary mortals into men of power. It brings power. It brings fire. It brings rain. It brings life. It brings God."
—Samuel Chadwick

SMALL GROUPS AND SUNDAY SCHOOL TEAM

This campaign is about transitioning people— getting them connected to God through connection with each other. In the end, we want healthy balanced churches, groups, and lives. This transition is accomplished through the use of small groups following the model of Acts 2:46-47:

"Every day they continued to meet together in the temple courts. They broke bread in their homes and ate together with glad and sincere hearts, praising God and enjoying the favor of all the people. And the Lord added to their number daily those who were being saved."

As Small Groups and Sunday School Team Coordinator, you will assume the role of Small Group Ministry Leader for the campaign. Your key roles, initially, are:

- Recruiting your team.

- Praying for your team.

Your key tasks for the campaign are:

- Recruiting Coaches who can provide support and direction to a group of small group hosts or Sunday School leaders. You will need adult, youth, and children's group Coaches.

- Recruiting small group hosts and/or Sunday School leaders. You will need adult, youth, and children's group hosts and Sunday School leaders.

- Connecting small group hosts and Sunday School leaders with a Coach and connecting Coaches with a Community Leader (the Community Leader level of small group management may not be applicable for all churches and can be combined with the Coach roles, where applicable).

- Recruiting two key team members. These are a Connection Events Coordinator and a Host and Leader Training Coordinator. Each of these leaders will need to build their own teams to manage their respective tasks as described later in this section.

- With the help of the Communication/Promotion Team Coordinator, developing promotional strategies and materials to promote events (Connections, Host Rally, Host Orientations, and team meetings).

- With the help of the Administrative Team, distributing promotional materials, small group curriculum (adult, youth, and children), and keeping records for all tiers of the Small Group Ministry (Community Leaders, Coaches, small group hosts, and member group assignments).

- Sponsoring a Host Rally four weeks before the first Connection event to gain commitment from existing small groups hosts, Sunday School leaders, and their apprentices, for the events of the campaign.

BUILDING YOUR TEAM

The make-up of your Small Groups and Sunday School Team will be more varied than some of the other teams in the campaign because you have a few major thrusts to manage:

- Building your Small Group Ministry by recruiting Coaches, and small group hosts and Sunday School leaders, if needed.

- Connecting new group members with small groups and Sunday School classes by hosting Connection events and providing on-site, web, and other opportunities for people to sign up for groups. Recruit a coordinator to manage this function as defined in the Connection Coordination section below.

- Resourcing and training new and existing leaders throughout the campaign. Recruit a coordinator to manage this function as defined in the Training for Leaders section below.

To handle these initiatives, your team should have a variety of people who collectively possess a combination of these skills:

- A heart for small groups and Sunday School classes for adults, youth, and children; Ability to recruit new small group hosts and Sunday School leaders;

- Good relationships with current leaders of small groups and Sunday School classes; Ability to prepare small group hosts to effectively lead their groups;

- Event planning and implementation skills; Training skills; and

- Ability to influence and inspire.

INVOLVEMENT BUILDS SUCCESS
Inviting people to play relatively small, but important, roles on your team increases energy, passion, knowledge, networking, creativity, influence, and ownership of the mission. Providing focused tasks, comprehensive training, and a wide variety of resources encourages volunteers to have a good experience and to perform their respective roles successfully.

THE TEAM
Two key team leaders will be needed on your team. These are a Connection Event Coordinator and a Host and Leader Training Coordinator. Each of these leaders will need to build their own teams to manage their respective tasks.

The key tasks for your Connection Events Coordinator are:

- To connect small group hosts and Sunday School leaders with a Coach and host Connection events to connect members to small groups.

- To provide on-site, web, and other opportunities for people to sign up for groups and connect new group members with small group hosts and Sunday School leaders. You will recruit adult, youth, and children's group members.

The key tasks for your Host and Leader Training Coordinator are:

- To resource and support new and existing groups throughout the campaign.

- To conduct host/leader orientations and training.

- To support and encourage small group hosts and Sunday School leaders through events and communication.

You probably already have an idea who you think would best fit in each of these roles. Pray over each role and choose people with the characteristics needed to fulfill the responsibilities of these roles.

Connection Events Coordinator:
The person in this role will build a team to develop the plan and oversee the implementation of the many elements of connecting people into small groups and Sunday School classes, including the Connection events.

Host and Leader Training Coordinator:
The person in this role will build a team to facilitate orientation and training of small group hosts and Sunday School leaders for adult, youth, and children's groups.

Once you have identified your team leaders, set to work building each team.

HOLD REGULAR MEETINGS
After you recruit your team, hold your first meeting. Communicate the main events timeline to the team and look over this Campaign Manual together to get yourselves on track. At the end of each meeting, spend time sharing your hearts for the campaign, praying for the team and the campaign, and committing to your next meeting date. We encourage you to spend time in the meeting working on each other's assignments together. This prevents isolation and promotes teamwork and accountability.

Begin holding monthly team meetings right away with whatever team members have been recruited. Then, once you are nine weeks out from the campaign, step it up to meeting every other week. Finally, in the five weeks before the campaign and for the six to seven weeks of the campaign, it might be wise for your team to meet weekly.

PRAY
Encourage your team to pray at every opportunity during planning and executing the events of the campaign.

SMALL GROUP MINISTRY LEADERSHIP MODEL

Developing a structure for leading your church's Small Group Ministry is an essential element in sustaining the small group movement in your church post-campaign. You will identify teams of Coaches to oversee up to 5-10 small group hosts each (up to 50-100 people in groups of 10 people).

The positions of Community Leader and Coach help fulfill the mission of the church by

1. Managing, ministering, and administering to the spiritual development of individuals and,

2. Encouraging the growth and expansion of their twenty or more small groups.

Under this model, a Coach disseminates information to the Small Group Ministry leadership and answers any questions or concerns within groups that the small group host is unable to handle. A Coach is usually selected from individuals who have demonstrated leadership skills inside or outside the church and are committed to the principle of doing small group life together. They cast vision for the community and are your shock absorbers, solving issues and problems as they arise.

The position of Coach helps fulfill the mission of the church by managing, ministering to, and administering the spiritual development of individuals and by insuring the growth and expansion of the small groups under them. The role of Coach is further defined below.

COACH ROLE FOR THE CAMPAIGN

Purpose:
Lead 5-10 small group hosts to encourage, motivate, and inspire them and their groups to have balanced spiritual health. Develop relationships with hosts to shepherd them to their next step.

Characteristics of the Coach. The Coach has a shepherd's **HEART**:
- **H**ands are open to God in service,
- **E**ncouraging to their small group hosts and group members,
- **A**vailable to minister and serve,
- **R**eluctant 'real' servant spirit (Moses, Peter), and
- **T**eachable for what God has for them in this role.

Responsibilities:

1. Provide shepherding to a few groups (up to five).

2. Be one step ahead and give hosts and leaders only one step at a time to keep them moving forward.

3. Connect with them regularly through:
   - One-on-one,

   - Visit the group (at least once during the campaign),

   - Huddle with them as leaders. Fellowship and socialize, if possible,
   - Email encouragement periodically, and

   - Call them or teleconference.

4. Cultivate the "health" of the small group hosts and group members through spiritual partners and mentors.

5. Coach groups to multiply.

SMALL GROUP HOST AND SUNDAY SCHOOL LEADER ROLE FOR THE CAMPAIGN

Purpose:
To create a community that builds the purposes of God deep within the hearts of every one of its members (Hebrews 10:24-25; Ephesians 2:19; Colossians 1:28).

Characteristics of the small group host or Sunday School leader:
A reluctant yet ready servant leader with a shepherd's heart. The small group host or Sunday School leader is a member of your church and growing spiritually.

Responsibilities:

- Bring people into community (membership) through the fellowship of a small group family and cultivate authentic relationships with one another (Hebrews 10:24-25; Ephesians 2:19).

- Build them up to maturity by cultivating the purposes of God in their lives and by helping them identify their spiritual next step (Colossians 1:28; Ephesians 4:15).

- Train them for ministry by giving every person a role or responsibility that helps mobilize them into ministry both inside and outside the group (Ephesians 4:11-13; 1 Corinthians 12:7; 1 Peter 3:10).

- Send them out for missions by motivating them to share their faith and ultimately spiritually reproduce their lives in others (either individually or as a group) (Matthew 28:18-20; Acts 20:24; 2 Timothy 2:2).

- Sustain them spiritually through by gathering them together for worship, prayer, devotions and communion (receiving care and coaching for leadership) (Romans 12:1-2; 1 Corinthians 15:58).

SMALL GROUPS OR SUNDAY SCHOOL?

It doesn't matter which one you do as long as you have heart-to-heart interaction. Both small groups and Sunday School classes are leadership factories and spaces for real spiritual growth.

Characteristics of each:

Small Groups	Sunday School
• Allow for longer fellowship time.	• Is convenient time-wise (worship and Bible study are held on the same day at the same time).
• Are more conducive to community.	• Has a convenient location.
• Have an infinitely expandable structure.	• Provides childcare.
• Demonstrate good stewardship—using homes so church facilities are not used.	• Makes managing the leadership easier.
• Are more likely to attract seekers.	

IDENTIFYING AND RECRUITING SMALL GROUP HOSTS AND SUNDAY SCHOOL LEADERS

Start With Prayer. Start by praying and asking God to reveal potential leaders. Jesus said, *"Ask the Lord of the Harvest to send out workers into His harvest field."* Matthew 9:38 (NIV)

THREE CRUCIAL LEADERSHIP QUESTIONS

Answering these three questions will bring clarity to your search for new small group hosts or Sunday School leaders for the campaign.

1. What do you need?

2. Who do you get?

3. Where do you find them?

QUESTION 1: WHAT DO YOU NEED?

You will need to recruit three sets of leaders to lead your church through the curriculum for this *Christian Life Trilogy*. You will need children's, youth, and adult small group hosts or Sunday School leaders. Whether you plan to organize groups into home-based small groups, or Sunday School classes, or both, you will need to first understand how many leaders and/or hosts you will need to recruit. You may want to check with the Campaign Director before finalizing these numbers, but this worksheet will give you a great starting point for your planning.

ADULT CALCULATIONS

A. Average number of adults in weekend attendance.	A =	500
B. Number of adults already connected in some kind of Small Group or Sunday School class.	B =	50
C. Subtract those in a group or class (B) from the average number of adults in weekend attendance (A).	A - B =	450
D. Divide the result (C) by group size to arrive at the number of short-term adult groups you could potentially start for the *Christian Life Trilogy*. This is also the number of new leaders you need to recruit.	C ÷ Group Size =	445

Not everyone will choose to participate in a small group or Sunday School class, but it will probably be more than you think. Because the small group component is a vital part of the overall campaign and you ask people for only a six to seven-week commitment (depending on the curriculum), you can expect a high percentage of participation.

CAUTION: You might conclude that starting 5, 10, or 20 new groups isn't possible because there isn't room in your building. Let this be a faith-stretching moment. Begin to think outside the box. Don't limit your options to the current times your groups meet or limit them to your church building. Pastor Rick Warren of Saddleback Church says, "Don't let the shoe tell the foot how big it can get."

So, don't let your building determine how many people you can place into a group. For adult groups, think of other places your groups could meet—offices, homes, or anywhere a DVD player can be set up.

QUESTION 2: WHO DO YOU GET?

Small group hosts and Sunday School leaders should be baptized members of your church. Look for people to be hosts and leaders of your small groups or Sunday School classes who have HEART:

- **H**onoring God with their lives. They don't have to be spiritual giants but they do need to be growing spiritually.

- **E**ncouraging. It is a great asset for the host or leader to be a warm-hearted person who is hospitable and makes people feel welcome and accepted.

- **A**vailable. You are asking for someone to host or lead a group for the six or seven weeks of the campaign.

- **R**eluctant. Be cautious of people who are overly eager to take on a group. Look for a humble, open, servant-hearted person.

- **T**eachable. They should be willing to learn and grow and be responsive to those in authority over them.

QUESTION 3: WHERE DO YOU FIND THESE LEADERS?

Consider people who you know have gifts of leadership, shepherding, encouragement, or teaching. So where do you look?

- Key Leaders. Look among the current church staff and key leaders serving in existing roles that might be willing to help with a group. It's a great opportunity to get some of your long time leaders on the front lines of ministry with some unconnected people.

- Current Small Group Hosts. Encourage existing group hosts to open their groups to new members for the campaign.

- Current Small Group Members. Encourage existing group hosts to release people from their group (who are members of the church, involved in ministry, and have demonstrated themselves to be rising leaders) to host a new campaign group. Since they have been experiencing group life, they are great candidates.

- Current Participants in Ministries. Look around in your church. Consider those who serve on committees, who are ushers or greeters, or those who work with missions or outreach. People who serve already can be relied on to understand and promote the value of community.

- Core Church Members. These people may not have an official leadership title, but they are involved and faithful.

- Pulpit Ask. Ask the Senior Pastor to 1) ask existing small group hosts or Sunday School leaders to commit to the campaign, and 2) to make a call for new small group hosts or Sunday School leaders during his or her sermons for the three weeks prior to the campaign: a "Campaign is Coming" pulpit announcement to recruit hosts. Make sure you have Host Commitment Cards available at the Information Table for people to fill out. We have found that baptized members of your church make the best small group hosts and Sunday School leaders. You will need to determine your list of qualifying questions, such as: "Are they a member of the church?" "Are they involved in ministry?" "Have they ever led a small group before?" or "Have they been baptized?" Then edit the template accordingly for your church.

- Connection Events. Small group host and Sunday School leader Connections are catalytic events during the campaign that will bring your people together to launch them into short-term groups. (This event is described in more detail in the Connection Coordination section later in this section, and you will see how some leaders are discovered and recruited at the Connection events.)

HOW TO CREATE NEW GROUPS

In prison, one of the harshest of punishments is solitary confinement. Cutting people off from relationship is painful. Yet, every weekend, churches are filled with people who are in a kind of solitary confinement.

One of the reasons that many Christians experience little spiritual growth and live defeated lives is that they are trying to live the Christian life in isolation. God never intended anyone to live the Christian life alone. Make it easy for people to sign up for small groups by offering several options:

1. Weekend Services.
   - Member Signup Bulletin Inserts
   - Information Table

2. In Person.
   - Sunday School classes
   - Ministry Offices

3. By Phone.

4. On the Web.

TWO FUNDAMENTAL CONVICTIONS

This campaign strongly champions the concept of connecting people into groups. Why? Two fundamental convictions form the foundation of this initiative:

1. Every Christian needs a spiritual family; and

2. Every sheep needs a shepherd.

As a result, one of the four commitments being asked of church members for the duration of the campaign is participation in the *Christian Life Trilogy* as part of a small group. (The other three commitments are to memorize a Scripture verse each week, read the devotional book, and hear all of the messages in the sermon series.) There is life-changing power in committing to a small group or Sunday School class campaign like this—don't underestimate it!

RALLYING YOUR CURRENT HOSTS AND LEADERS

The first step to take when starting to recruit hosts for the new groups you want to form for the *Christian Life Trilogy* is to hold a Host Rally. Invite existing hosts, leaders, and their apprentices. The purpose of the meeting is to gain buy-in for the events of the campaign and give leaders a heads-up about what is coming. This will be the time to encourage leaders to put their current studies on hold for the campaign and open their groups to new people. When inviting hosts and leaders to the Host Rally, ask them to bring the prospective leaders in their groups to the meeting as well.

EXPANDING EXISTING GROUPS
Existing small group hosts are encouraged to expand their groups for the duration of the campaign. Small group hosts can use the **Circles of Life** in their groups to identify people they could invite to their groups. Hand these out to leaders at the Host Rally and the Host Orientation meetings held just before each of the Connection events.

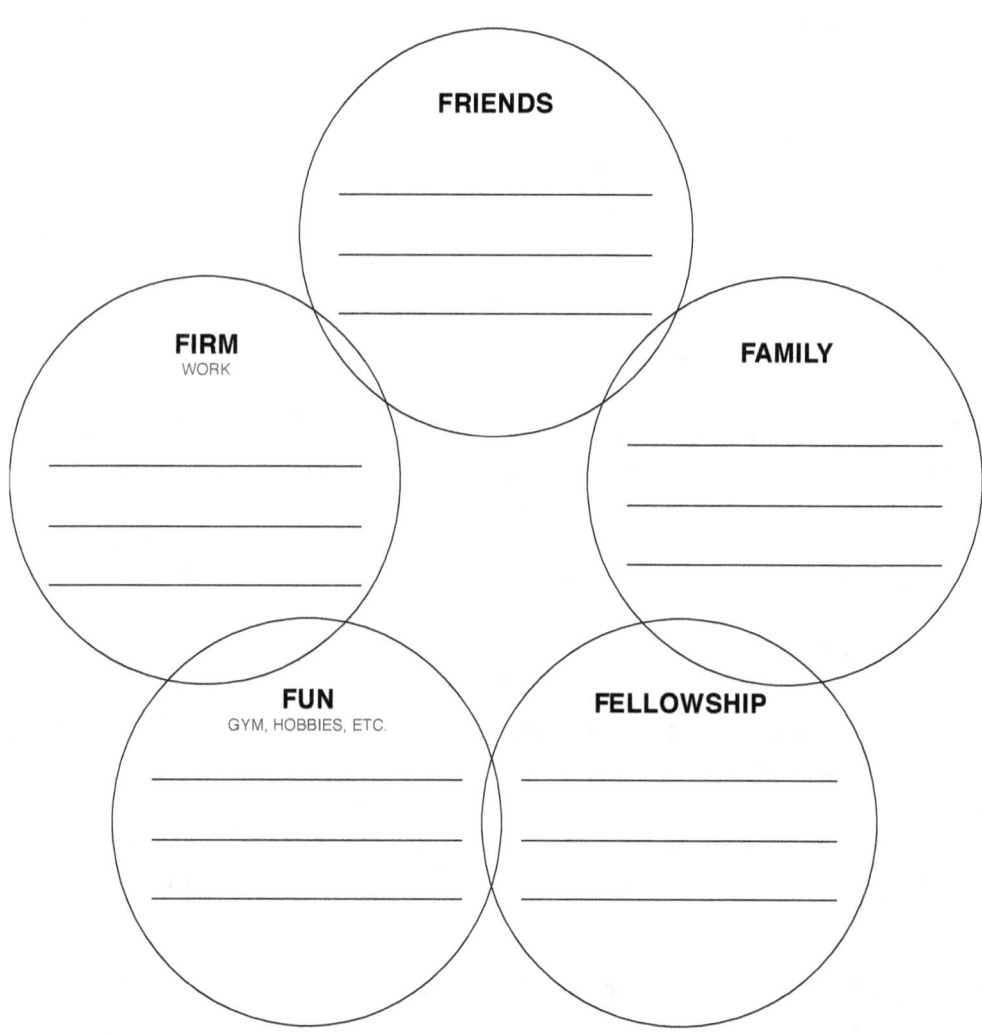

CONNECTING MEMBERS TO SMALL GROUPs

In addition to shifting your current small groups or Sunday School classes to the *Christian Life Trilogy* curriculum during the campaign, you will need to provide connections for those who are currently unconnected to a small group or Sunday School class. It is important to provide easy, quick methods for people to sign up to attend a small group or Sunday School class. You will accommodate sign-up by phone, email, in person, sign- up cards, and web, where applicable.

SMALL GROUP MANAGEMENT AND RECORDKEEPING

Your church will benefit from a software solution for connecting and tracking your Small Group Ministry information. If you already have a software solution in place, great! If not, work with the Connection Events Coordinator and Administrative Team Coordinator to evaluate current software such as ChurchTeams' online GroupFinder with built-in mapping software (www.churchteams.com).

Once the processes are in place, you should work with the Administrative Team Coordinator to track your Small Group Ministry leaders, small group hosts, and members for small group sign-up and management.

TOOLS

Curricula: The *Christian Life Trilogy* curriculum has been published in three studies—The Crucified Life, The Resurrected Life, and The Spirit-filled Life.

Adult Small Groups or Sunday School Classes, Video-Based Study: Using this curriculum, small groups view a teaching segment on DVD, then follow with group discussion, prayer, and worship using the study guide for each of the three parts of the series: The Crucified Life, The Resurrected Life, and The Spirit-filled Life. Each of the three series has a daily Devotional Book that aligns with the weekly study and encourages personal application. Each participant should receive both a study guide and a daily devotional book. These study guides and devotional books are available for purchase in booklet form.

http://christianlifetrilogy.com

www.ingramcontent.com/pod-product-compliance
Lightning Source LLC
Chambersburg PA
CBHW051423070526
44584CB00023B/3561